WAITING FOR JESUS

by Beatrice (Bea) Cunningham

DORRANCE
PUBLISHING CO
EST. 1920
PITTSBURGH, PENNSYLVANIA 15238

Dorrance Publishing Co
585 Alpha Drive
Pittsburgh, PA 15238
Visit our website at www.dorrancebookstore.com

ISBN: 978-1-6366-1261-4
EISBN: 978-1-6366-1847-0

They who wait, trust, hope in the Lord shall renew their strength. They shall mount up on wings like an eagle. They shall run and not grow weary. They shall walk and not faint.

Isaiah 40:31

Teach us, Lord, teach us, Lord, how to wait.

TABLE OF CONTENTS

DEDICATION

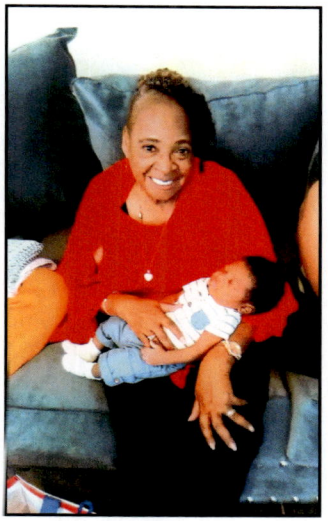

This book is dedicated to our granddaughter, Alexis C. Thomas who assisted me with the typing and to Azariah G. Hobbs, who was such a good baby while his mother was typing.

Acknowledgments

I would like to thank our daughters and all of our grandchildren who are always so helpful and available to me. I thank them for the times they planned things for me, spent time with me, and brought me supplies and gifts. This has encouraged and helped me to complete this project.

INTRODUCTION

The concept, goal and dream to write this book began during the Advent Season as I would go daily into the chapel of the senior care community where I live. I was drawn to the decorations in front of the altar. There was an empty manger surrounded by hay and an adult sheep and a little lamb. The adult sheep was seated and always seemed to be at peace, while the little lamb stood on all four legs with mouth opened as if he/she had something to say or questions to ask. I began to hear the little lamb speak and ask questions, like, "Why is the manger empty?" "Where is the baby?"

I began to hear the adult sheep peacefully talking to the little lamb about how we must prepare for the coming of Jesus. As we wait for Jesus to come, we are not passive but should be actively doing those things that will help us to be prepared for His coming. I thought to myself what a wonderful idea to let the adult sheep tell the little lamb ways to prepare for the coming of Jesus as we all await His coming. Jesus is going to come soon and very soon to the world, especially for those who have prepared for His coming. The bride prepares for her wedding by doing so many things and Jesus is coming for His bride (those who have prepared themselves). We prepare ourselves for the coming of Jesus not only during Advent but every day of our lives. For Jesus can come at any time, this may even be the day.

Therefore, each day the adult sheep will tell the little lamb ways to open up his/her heart to Jesus and grow in the Spirit. The first step being to surrender our lives to Him, so that with the help of His Spirit in us we can be ready to live in a way that is pleasing to Jesus. Our lives will be dedicated to Him and we will follow Him in making our everyday decisions and actions.

The book of Proverbs was used by Ancient Israel to teach God's people how to live a life pleasing to God. It will be used as a resource to talk to the little lamb and to us about things we can do to get prepared as we await the coming of Jesus. Each day the little lamb and the readers will receive wisdom from the scripture and conversations. We need to remember that wisdom is a gift from God and the greatest gift of all is Jesus. God so loved the world that He gave His only begotten Son to us so that we could be saved.

In the preparation for each day the assigned scriptures will be read by the adult sheep who will lead the activities of the day. The paper strips, index card, or poster with the memory verse for the day will be made before beginning each day and ready for use.

Then the day will begin with a prayer song to the Holy Spirit to lead them and guide them. St. Augustine says, "When we sing, we pray twice." That is why we suggest singing the opening and closing prayers. You may use any rhythm or tune that comes to mind. You are asking the Holy Spirit to lead you as you begin the activities of each day. The Holy Spirit will give us the wisdom we need to come to Jesus and let Him live His life in us. The Holy Spirit will help the little lamb and the readers to make wise decisions and grow in wisdom, knowledge, and in favor with God and man. This book is very interactive, with activities to assist the little lamb and the adult sheep to participate and add their own uniqueness to the suggested prayers and activities.

First, the family should set up a Prayer Heritage Table. The table should have a Bible enthroned with a cross and any other items that are a part of the family's heritage. The person who will be the adult sheep and read the book with the little lamb(s) should read the scripture assigned for each day, in which the memory verse is contained and prepare the memory verse on paper strips, index cards, or poster *before* beginning the activities of the day. The scripture for each day and instructions for memorization of the scripture is highlighted in green in the introduction. The green color represents growth and the word of God helps us to grow and become strong, wise, and to flourish.

Each day will begin with this prayer that should be sung to any tune or rhythm you decide.

COME, HOLY SPIRIT. COME, HOLY SPIRIT. COME, HOLY SPIRIT. COME AND LEAD US TODAY.

Then, the memorization of the memory verse for the day will begin. They are taken from your family Bible after the adult sheep read the whole chapter where they are contained. Then the memory verse should be written on strips of paper, index cards, or poster. The verse will be read many times until the little lamb can recite the memory verse without the paper or poster. The technique is to fold back or cover one word at a time, reading the verse with everyone saying all the words in the verse. You are to fold back or cover the words one at a time until the verse can be said without the help of the written strips, index cards, or poster. The memory verse should be read from the family Bible before beginning the memorization activity. Make it fun not stressful.

The conversation between the adult sheep and little lamb begins after the memory verse activity. The memory verse should be read from the family Bible. If your child can read, let them read the parts of the little lamb. The parts spoken by the little lamb is highlighted in purple. Purple is the color of royalty and our children need to be reminded that they are children of God, children of the King, adopted children of God.

When the conversation ends each day, the adult sheep may add a personal sharing or testimony. This should be kept very short and leads to the closing prayer together. The beginning of the prayer is in the book with space for the adult leader or group to add their own prayer intentions.

Each day ends with the Closing Prayer Song:

COME, LORD JESUS. COME, LORD JESUS. COME, LORD JESUS. COME AND BE BORN IN OUR HEARTS.

On the 25th day you will have a birthday party for Jesus after your daily activities. You are encouraged to invite friends and family to the party. Have fun and games as you would at any party. The scripture reading about the birth of Jesus will be included.

It is so important that we open our hearts and lives to Jesus and as we share these activities, scriptures and prayers with our children, this will help them become stronger Christians with the ability to make wise decisions and to take a stand for the Lord and do what is right. We live in a world where the spiritual warfare is being battled and our children must know that the closer they get to Jesus the more victorious they will be. These daily reminders of how we can grow in the Spirit will help us all to put on the armor of God. Jesus is coming to receive those who are prepared and waiting for Him to come. COME, LORD JESUS!

PREPARATION DAY

Your heritage table should be set up with the Holy Bible enthroned. On this preparation day read John chapter 3 from your family Bible. Make the memory verse strips, index cards, or poster with the words from John 3:16. This is such a well-known verse that your family may already know. Make the paper strips, index cards, or poster and use the time to practice on the procedure for memorization of the verse. Always read the memory verse from your family Bible. The procedure for memorization of the scripture is in the introduction and is highlighted in green. Then the conversation between the adult sheep and the little lamb begins. If your child can read, let them read the parts of the little lamb. The adult sheep will be given an opportunity to add personal comments at the end of the conversations and add to the ending of the closing prayers. It will make the activities more meaningful to your little lambs as you share your insights and/or personal testimony of your faith in Jesus. The symbol /// indicates that you are to sing the verse three times.

Begin with the Prayer song:

COME, HOLY SPIRIT. COME, HOLY SPIRIT. COME, HOLY SPIRIT. COME AND LEAD US TODAY.

Read John 3:16 from your family Bible. Follow the instructions for memorization of scripture that is highlighted in green in the introduction. When the little lamb(s) have been successful in repeating the memory verse with little or no help, the conversation begins. If your child can read, let them read the parts of the little lamb.

Adult sheep: We are waiting for the coming of the Baby Jesus. When we have a special event or guest coming, we clean, decorate, and prepare the house for their coming. We are now in the time when we are waiting for Jesus to come. We, too, must do some things to get ready for Jesus.

Little lamb: What are we going to do to get ready?

We are going to actively wait as we tidy up our mind, body, and spirit and be ready to let Jesus come in and lead us to a closer walk with God, His Father. Jesus is the Son of God! He was born in a manger because there was no room for Him in the inn. The people were not prepared for His coming. He wasn't born in a castle or stately home but in a cave where the animals were kept as He identified with the poor and neglected children of the world. He took the form of a little baby, depending on others for all of His needs, just as all babies do. The Bible says He came with a mission and the mission was to save all people from sin and destruction. He came unto His own people, but they did not accept Him. But to those who did accept Him, He gave them the power to become children of God. He asked us to believe in His name and in the Father who sent Him.

Remember our memory verse, "For God so loved the world that He gave His only Son, so that everyone who believes in Him might not perish but have eternal life."

Therefore, as we wait for the coming of Jesus, we can say to God the Father, "We believe in your Son, Jesus, and we are preparing to let Him come and save us. We welcome Jesus into our hearts, into our home, and into our lives. God loves us and gives us grace from the Holy Spirit to help us grow in wisdom, in knowledge, and in favor with God and man. As we wait, we will learn and put into practice many ways to draw closer to Jesus. I remember when I first came to believe in Jesus. (Add your personal testimony or comments.)

Let's pray together: Lord Jesus, we await your coming today, tomorrow, or at the end of time. We welcome you into our home, our hearts, our lives. We ask the Holy Spirit to pour out His Spirit upon us and help us to listen, to obey, and grow in the Spirit. (Add your own prayers, and then end with the prayer song.)

COME, LORD JESUS. COME, LORD JESUS. COME, LORD JESUS. COME AND BE BORN IN OUR HEARTS.

DAY 1

Preparation: Read Proverbs chapter one and write the memory verse on paper strips, index cards, or poster with the words from Proverbs chapter 1 verse 33. The book of Proverbs has so much wisdom to offer and some themes are throughout the book. You will read one chapter at a time from Proverbs and will concentrate on and include ideas and insights from the memory verses. There will be time at the end of the conversations between the adult sheep and the little lamb to add any input that the Holy Spirit gives to you. This should be short, and if possible, should be a personal testimony. You will also be given an opportunity to add to the closing prayer each day.

The memory verse for today is: Proverbs chapter 1: verse 33. Read the memory verse from your family Bible.

Use the instructions on how to teach the memory verses that is highlighted in green in the introduction. When you both can repeat the memory verse without the help of the paper strips, index cards, or poster, the conversation begins between the adult sheep and the little lamb. If any of the children in your home or group can read, ask them if they would like to read the parts of the little lamb. If not, the adult sheep reads the parts in a different voice.

Begin with the prayer song:

COME, HOLY SPIRIT. COME, HOLY SPIRIT. COME, HOLY SPIRIT. COME AND LEAD US TODAY. ///

Read the memory verse from your family Bible, Proverbs chapter 1 verse 33. Use the procedure for memorization of scriptures highlighted in green in the introduction to assist in memorization of the scripture verse. Then the conversation between the adult sheep and the little lamb begins.

6

Adult sheep: To be ready and open to instruction with fear and reverence of the Lord is the beginning of wisdom. Children who listen to their father's instruction, their mother's teaching, and obey God will live in security, in peace, without fear or harm.

Little lamb: I remember we talked about God's love shown to us through Jesus, His Son, and we prayed to let Jesus come into our hearts. Now what do we do?

Adult sheep: We respond to God's love with an attitude of gratitude. We thank God for Jesus and we strive to wait in peace doing the right things. You should listen to your parents' teaching and do not let others lead you to do things that you know are wrong. Do not strive for money dishonestly and be grateful to God for all that you already have. When you obey instructions and seek wisdom and knowledge, you will dwell in security, in peace, without fear or harm. Jesus Christ brings to us spiritual blessings from heaven. God is so kind and decided that Jesus would choose us to be God's own adopted children. Jesus Christ came as a little baby born out of God's love for us. He came to save us from sin and destruction. He sacrificed His life for us on the Cross to set us free, which means that our sins are forgiven.

Little lamb: I am so grateful for God's love and I want to get ready for Jesus. What else can I do?

Adult sheep: You can pray and listen to God's word and obey the teachings that you receive. For the Lord God gives wisdom and from His mouth comes knowledge and understanding. I remember when I was growing up and learned a valuable lesson. (Add your personal testimony.)

Let us pray now and ask God to help us prepare for the coming of Jesus every day.

We pray together, Lord Jesus, thank you and praise you for coming to save us. For coming as a little baby so helpless and depending on your mother and father showing us that we should be humble and rely on God. Help us to listen to our parents and follow God's way of love. Holy Spirit help us, lead us to make good decisions and do what is right. (Add you own conclusion to the prayer and end with the closing prayer song.)

COME, LORD JESUS. COME, LORD JESUS. COME, LORD JESUS. COME AND BE BORN IN OUR HEARTS.

DAY 2

Preparation: Read Chapter 2 of Proverbs and make the paper strips, index cards, or poster with the words from Proverbs chapter 2 verse 6. After the opening prayer song use the procedure for memorization of scripture highlighted in green in the introduction of the book to help memorize the scripture of the day. Then the conversation begins between the mother sheep and the baby lamb.

Opening prayer song:

COME, HOLY SPIRIT. COME, HOLY SPIRIT. COME, HOLY SPIRIT. COME AND LEAD US TODAY.

Read the memory verse Proverbs: chapter 2 verse 6, from your family Bible. Use the procedure for memorization of the scriptures highlighted in green in the introduction to help your little lamb remember the memory verse for today.

Adult sheep: What do you hear from the scripture today?

Little lamb: I heard that if I ask God for help to wait and want to become wise, He will help me.

Adult sheep: Yes, you are smart and intelligent, but do not rely on your own intelligence, trust in God and seek His way of doing things. Make your decisions based on what God would want you to do. Jesus came to show us the way to the Father and how to live as we wait for His return. We are waiting on Jesus now, realizing He could come any day. We win favor with God when we love the Lord Jesus and strive to be faithful to His teachings. When we turn away from evil and do good, God makes our paths straight and we will be healthy, have energy, and live a happier life. Long life is promised to children who honor and obey their parents. Also, when you obey God and follow His ways, you will be able, with God's presence and help, to overcome fear and sleep in peace. There will be no monsters underneath your bed. Jesus is your confidence and protector, and He will keep you in perfect peace as you keep your mind on him.

We have the Holy Spirit who comes to us and helps us to make good decisions as we await the coming of Jesus. The Spirit will make you wise and help you understand what it means to know God through His Son, Jesus Christ. That is why we begin each day with our prayer song asking the Holy Spirit to come and lead us. (Add your comments or testimony. Keep comments short.)

Let us pray together: Come, Holy Spirit help us and let your light shine in our hearts to help us make room for Jesus in our everyday lives. Help us to rely on God and make decisions based on what we learn from God's word. (Add your own prayers and petitions, then conclude with the Closing Prayer Song.)

COME, LORD JESUS. COME, LORD JESUS. COME, LORD JESUS. COME AND BE BORN IN OUR HEARTS.

DAY 3

Preparation: Read Proverbs chapter 3 then make the paper strips, index cards, or poster with the words from Proverbs chapter 3: verse 5. Review the procedure for memorization of scripture highlighted in green in the introduction.

Opening prayer song:

COME, HOLY SPIRIT. COME, HOLY SPIRIT. COME, HOLY SPIRIT. COME AND LEAD US TODAY. ///

Now, read the memory verse Proverbs chapter 2: verse 5 from your family Bible. Use the procedure for memorization to teach the memory verse to your little lamb.

Adult sheep: God has promised us many things as we place our trust in him. If we are mindful of him, He will direct our paths and make them straight. Always let God lead you and He will clear the road for you to follow. You will find favor with God and learn to trust Him even more. As we wait for Jesus to come, if we rely on Him and not our own intelligence, your hearts will be more open and you will be ready for His coming. Do not turn away or become bitter when the Lord corrects you. The Lord corrects everyone He loves.

Little lamb: I like the part about finding favor, but I am not so sure about the correction part.

Adult sheep: When we are corrected, it helps us to become wise and make good choices. If we are never corrected when we do wrong, these will become bad habits and lead to sin. Don't ever think that you are wise enough, but respect the Lord and stay away from evil. Use common sense and sound judgment; this will make you wise, strong, and healthy. It will help you to live a long life and be better prepared for Jesus when He comes. (Add your comments or personal testimony.)

Let us pray together: Lord Jesus, Father, Holy Spirit help us to make good decisions and rely on God. Help us to trust in the Lord with all of our heart as we await the coming of Jesus. When we are corrected, let us see the love that is there and strive to do better. (Add your own prayers and then conclude with the closing prayer song.)

COME, LORD JESUS. COME, LORD JESUS. COME, LORD JESUS. COME AND BE BORN IN OUR HEARTS.

DAY 4

In preparation for the day, read Proverbs Chapter 4 and make the paper strips, index cards, or poster with the memory verses, Proverbs chapter 4: verse 4. Begin the day with the opening prayer song.

COME, HOLY SPIRIT. COME, HOLY SPIRIT. COME, HOLY SPIRIT. COME AND LED US TODAY.

Read the memory verses from your family Bible, Proverbs chapter 4: verse 4. Use the procedure for memorization of scripture, highlighted in green in the introduction to help your little lamb remember the scripture verse for the day.

Adult sheep: As we wait for Jesus to come, there are benefits in taking the time to learn more about how to wait and receive wisdom.

Little lamb: Benefits? What benefits?

Adult sheep: There are many negative things that happen to children in this world; wisdom will safeguard you and show you the way to go. Making decisions based on sound judgment, and the word of God will help you live a long and happy life. Wisdom will bring you honors if you embrace her and the teachings from the word of God. God's word is a lamp unto our feet, a light unto our paths. You must choose to walk in the light of the Holy Spirit, in the light of God's word. When we take the word of God to heart, we speak and act with wisdom. Yes, Jesus is coming to receive those who are walking in the light and ready like a bride for her wedding feast. God loves us just the way we are, but He is coming for those who are ready and prepared for His coming.

(You may add a personal testimony or comments.)

Let us continue to pray together and ask for the grace that we need to become ready for Jesus to come. Holy Spirit give us the grace to hide God's word in our hearts and let its instruction come out in the way we live our lives. Help us to make good choices that will bring us closer to Jesus and ready for His coming. (You may add your prayers here.)

Let us sing our closing prayer song together:

COME, LORD JESUS. COME, LORD JESUS. COME, LORD JESUS. COME AND BE BORN IN OUR HEARTS.

DAY 5

Preparation: Read Proverbs chapter 5 and prepare the paper strips, index cards, or poster with the memory verse, Proverbs: chapter 5, verse 1.

Begin with the opening prayer song:

COME, HOLY SPIRIT. COME, HOLY SPIRIT. COME, HOLY SPIRIT. COME AND LEAD US TODAY.

Read the memory verse from your family Bible, Proverbs chapter 5: verse 1. Use the procedure for memorization of scripture highlighted in green in the introduction to help your little lamb(s) remember the memory verse for the day.

Adult sheep: As we are waiting for Jesus to come, we strive to get understanding. This understanding and knowledge will be your guard. It will help you in all areas of your life and help you to choose the right kind of friends.

Little lamb: I thought we are to love everybody!

Adult sheep: Yes, God is love and we are to love God with all our heart, mind, body and will. Jesus also said, "We should love our neighbor as we love ourselves." As you love everybody, you must listen to the voice of wisdom and not let anyone influence you to do wrong things. If you have a friend who keeps getting himself and you into trouble, it is time to let go of that person and make new friends. You are to listen to the voice of your parents and teachers and obey instruction. The Lord knows and sees all things. The wicked will be caught in the midst of their own sins and bad choices. They will get into trouble because of a lack of discipline, lost because of their own foolish decisions.

What a friend we have in Jesus! He is always available to us and wants to keep us on the right track. That's another reason why we prepare as we wait for Jesus. We want to be ready, doing the right things when He comes. (You may add a personal testimony or comments here.)

Everyone is always free to choose their activities and friends, let us together pray and ask the Holy Spirit to help us make the correct choices and be ready when Jesus comes.

Holy Spirit, grant us the wisdom to make the right choices in life. Help us to be ready when Jesus comes. Help us to choose good friends and to love all people. Help us to listen to the voices of our parents, teachers and all those who love us and love God. (Add your prayers)

Closing prayer song:

COME, LORD JESUS. COME, LORD JESUS. COME, LORD JESUS. COME AND BE BORN IN OUR HEARTS.

DAY 6

Preparation: Read Proverbs chapter 6. Then make your paper strips, index cards, or poster with the memory verse Proverbs chapter 6: verse 6.

Begin with the opening prayer song:

COME, HOLY SPIRIT. COME, HOLY SPIRIT. COME, HOLY SPIRIT. COME AND LEAD UD TODAY.

Read the memory verse from your family Bible, Proverbs chapter 6: verse 6. Use the procedure for memorization of scripture, highlighted in green in the introduction. When the little lamb has done a good job of memorizing the scripture, the conversation between the adult sheep and the little lamb begins.

Adult sheep: Do you have any questions about the memory verse?

Little lamb: Yes, why all this talk about ants?

Adult sheep: While we are waiting for Jesus to come, we are to be like the ants. We are to be busy doing simple things in loving ways and we should not have to always be reminded to do good, we should do good because it is the right thing to do. For though, no one is telling the ants what to do they are preparing on their own for the winter months when food will be hard to find. Like the ants storing what they will need later on, if we make it a habit to choose good over evil and form good habits, this will become easier and more easier to do. We will be better prepared for Jesus's coming.

Little lamb: I am going to be like the ants busy preparing for Jesus to come. So that even when things get tough, I will strive to make good choices.

Adult sheep: Yes, it is better to strive to do God's will everyday so that it becomes the way we live our lives. God loves us just the way we are, and He gives grace and mercy to help us grow in wisdom, in stature and in favor with God and man. (Add comments or personal testimony.)

Pray together: Come, Holy Spirit and help us to make good habits by doing everyday activities with love. Help us to be like the ants, preparing for tomorrow by what we do on today. (Add your own prayers.)

Closing prayer song:

COME, LORD JESUS. COME, LORD JESUS. COME, LORD JESUS. COME AND BE BORN IN OUR HEARTS.

DAY 7

Preparation: Read to yourself Proverbs chapter 7. Make the memory verse strips, index cards, or poster with the words from Proverbs chapter 7: verse 2.

Then begin with the opening prayer song:

COME, HOLY SPIRIT. COME, HOLY SPIRIT. COME, HOLY SPIRIT. COME AND LEAD US TODAY.

Read the memory verse Proverbs chapter 7: verse 2 from your family Bible. Use the procedure for memorization to help your little lamb (s) remember the memory verse for today.

Adult sheep: As the memory verse states you are to pay close attention to the instructions you are given. Obey them and you will live a long, happy life.

Little lamb: I know I am waiting, and listening, why is it taking so long?

Adult sheep: Waiting should not be a time when we sit around and complain or do nothing. It is the time to put into practice those things we are learning about how to wait. First, the right attitude while we are waiting is very important. We are to think positively and keep God's word and follow His commands. Let the word of God be on your mind and in your heart. You will be wiser and wiser and you will begin to enjoy your time of waiting. You will begin to realize what a treasure you are acquiring and where your treasure is that is where your heart will be also. You will realize that you are being better prepared to meet the Lord Jesus. The wisdom you receive will help you to keep away from people, places and things that will lead you into trouble and sin. God loves us and has a time and plan for when Jesus will come. No one knows the day or the hour therefore we should stay prepared and ready for Jesus to come. We show our love for God and Jesus by being obedient to God's commands and treasuring His word. (Add your comments or personal testimony.)

Let us pray together and ask the Holy Spirit to help us. Holy Spirit we want to be ready when Jesus comes. Help us to be ready with the right attitude. Lord Jesus we want to be more like you, help us to grow more and more into your image and likeness. (Add your own prayers.)

Closing prayer song:

COME, LORD JESUS. COME, LORD JESUS. COME, LORD JESUS. COME AND BE BORN IN OUR HEARTS.

Day 8

Preparation: Read Proverbs chapter 8 and prepare the memory verse on the paper strips, index cards, or poster. The memory verse is Proverbs chapter 8: verse 7.

Begin with the opening prayer song:

COME, HOLY SPIRIT. COME, HOLY SPIRIT. COME, HOLY SPIRIT. COME AND LEAD US TODAY. ///

Read Proverbs chapter 8: verse 7 from your family Bible. Use the procedure for memorization of scripture highlighted in green in the introduction to help memorize the memory verse for today.

Adult sheep: As we wait for the coming of Jesus there are some virtues we need to develop and one to them is to be honest.

Little lamb: To be honest means to tell the truth. What does that have to do with the Coming of Jesus?

Adult sheep: We talked about how Jesus is coming and no one knows the day or hour but we must be prepared. Honesty is very important and wisdom teaches us to tell the truth. It is wise to speak the truth and do not lie, as we wait for Jesus to come. Understanding will help us to see that we need the word of God to direct our lives. We should let instruction and knowledge mean more to us than riches, finest gold or silver. If you pay attention to what you are taught from the word of God, God will help you plan and wait and you will be happy.

Wisdom from the word of God helps us to be truthful and honest in our words and deeds. We really show that we are growing in wisdom when we can control our lips and tongue. We should not be deceitful and try to fool people, but be sincere and do not be crooked. If you say you are going to do something, keep your word. Do not swear at all, answer yes or no and be honest.

Jesus loves us just as we are, but He calls us to grow and change to become a better person. This takes time and there is always more to learn and put into practice. We are on a journey and the journey gets sweeter every day as you wait for Jesus and become more like him. You are a precious child of God made in His image and likeness. God has a special place prepared for you. (Add your personal testimony or comments.)

Let us pray together and ask the Holy Spirit to help us. Holy Spirit as we wait for the coming of Jesus help us to be honest and to grow in the spirit. Help us to control our mouth and tongue and be honest in all that we do. Help us to listen to God's word and put the word into practice in our lives. Help us to know that becoming wise is more important than getting the world's richest because wisdom will help us to be happy and overcome evil with good. (Add your personal prayers.)

Closing prayer song:

COME, LORD JESUS. COME, LORD JESUS. COME, LORD JESUS. COME AND BE BORN IN OUR HEARTS.

DAY 9

Preparation: Read Proverbs chapter 9 and prepare the memory verse on strips of paper, index cards, or poster. The memory verse for today is Proverbs chapter 9: verse 10.

Opening prayer song:

COME, HOLY SPIRIT. COME, HOLY SPIRIT. COME, HOLY SPIRIT. COME AND LEAD US TODAY.

Read the memory verse Proverbs chapter 9: verse 10 from your family Bible. Complete the memory verse activity as explained in the introduction, highlighted in green.

Adult sheep: What we are doing as we wait on Jesus is very important. We are receiving instruction that will help us to have even better sense and know more about the value of being corrected. So that when we are corrected, we will see the love that is attached to it. This will help you become wiser with a long, happy, life with a good reputation. We should always remember that the fear of the God is the beginning of wisdom. To really get to know God we must strive to get understanding and forsake the foolish so that we may live a peaceful happy life.

Little lamb: I want to have a long happy life and I also want Jesus to come right away.

Adult sheep: I want to be happy and I want Jesus to come also. That is why we are spending this time together each day, learning about how to become wiser as we wait for Jesus to come. We also pray and ask for the help of the Holy Spirit because we need the guidance of the Holy Spirit in our lives. To live a long happy life we are to listen, pray and actively let the Spirit of God lead us. (Add your comments or personal testimony.)

Adult sheep: Let us pray together: Lord Jesus, we are actively waiting for you to come. Give us more wisdom, knowledge and understanding as we spend this time with you. We know that you love us and is always with us and that you want us to become more and more like you every day. Help us to listen, to pray, to make good choices and do the right things. (Add your own prayers.)

Closing prayer song:

COME, LORD JESUS. COME, LORD JESUS. COME, LORD JESUS. COME AND BE BORN IN OUR HEARTS.

DAY 10

Preparation: Read Proverbs chapter 10 and prepare the memory verse strips, index cards, or poster with the words from Proverbs chapter 10: verse 2.

Begin the day with the opening prayer song:

COME, HOLY SPIRIT. COME, HOLY SPIRIT. COME, HOLY SPIRIT. COME AND LEAD US TODAY.

Read Proverbs chapter 10: verse 2 from your family Bible. Use the procedure for memorization of scripture found in the green highlighted area of the introduction to learn the memory verse.

Adult sheep: Waiting is not just sitting around and doing nothing. It is doing the things that will make those around you happy instead of being sad.

Little lamb: I know how I can make my parents happy. I can obey them right away, and not have them having to tell me over and over what to do.

Adult sheep: Yes, this is very important and it could save your life. If your parent or the person in charge, sees danger coming and tells you what to do, and you do not listen, you could be putting your life in danger. A good practice is to stop, listen, and obey right away.

Also do not be dishonest and make bad decisions about money and material gain. What you gain by doing evil won't help you at all, but being good can save you from death. It is smart to work hard for what you want. Store up treasure in heaven by making good decisions and choosing to do what Jesus would do. Remember only what we do for Christ will last and have us ready when Jesus comes. This will also lead us to eternal life and to our heavenly home. (Add your comments or testimony.)

Let us pray, Holy Spirit come and help us to be obedient and follow the example of Jesus as He did the will of His Father. Help us to obey those who are in authority, like our parents and teachers. Help us to not be lazy but to work for those things that we want and prepare for the future. (Add your own prayers, then conclude with the closing prayer song.)

COME, LORD JESUS. COME, LORD JESUS. COME, LORD JESUS. COME AND BE BORN IN OUR HEARTS.

DAY 11

Preparation: Read Proverbs Chapter 11 and make the memory verse strips, index cards, or poster with the memory verse, Proverbs 11: verse 12.

Begin with the opening prayer song:

COME, HOLY SPIRIT. COME, HOLY SPIRIT. COME, HOLY SPIRIT. COME AND BE BORN IN OUR HEARTS.

Read the memory verse Proverbs chapter 11: verse 12 from your family Bible. Use the procedure for memorization of scripture highlighted in green in the introduction to help memorize Proverbs 11: verse 12.

Adult sheep: As we wait for Jesus to come, we are to not say bad things about others and we are not to gossip. When someone tells you bad things about others, let the gossip end with you, tell it to no one. We can pray and ask the Lord for a clean heart and know that those who do evil will be punished. Some people think that they have gotten away with evil because no one saw what they did. God knows and sees all things.

Little lamb: As I wait for Jesus, I want to do what is right.

Mother sheep: We have the Holy Spirit within us to help us make good choices and that is why we begin each day with our prayer song, "Come, Holy Spirit." Jesus is our true friend and we are to take everything to God in prayer. We also need wise leaders to help our cities not to end up in ruin. They make decisions that will affect others and need to have wisdom from God to say and do the right things. A lack of guidance may cause people to fail and in making decisions sometimes you may need many counselors. There will be many situations in our lives where there are many ideas surfacing and our leaders are telling us different ways to address the issues and we are trying to determine who to listen to. This is when we are to go to God in prayer and listen to the God within us. (Add your comments or testimony.)

Let us pray together: O God, let the Holy Spirit who proceeds from you enlighten our minds and help to make the right decisions and lead us to perfect truth. As we wait for Jesus to come help us to overcome evil by doing good. (Add your own prayers, then conclude with the closing prayer song.)

COME, LORD JESUS. COME, LORD
JESUS. COME, LORD JESUS. COME
AND BE BORN IN OUR HEARTS.

DAY 12

Preparation: Read Proverbs chapter 12 and prepare the memory verse strips, index cards, or poster with the memory verse, Proverbs 12: 16

Opening prayer song:

COME, HOLY SPIRIT. COME, HOLY SPIRIT. COME, HOLY SPIRIT. COME AND LEAD US TODAY.

Begin the memory verse activity by reading Proverbs 12:16 from your family Bible. The procedure is highlighted in green in the introduction.

Adult sheep: Careless words can cause many misunderstandings so we are to think before we speak as we wait for Jesus to come. People will say and do things that make us angry we are not to respond in anger, ignoring an insult can be the smart thing to do.

Little lamb: Won't people think that they can take advantage of me, if I let them insult or bully me?

Adult sheep: This is where the Holy Spirit comes into the situation. When we are still and let the Lord fight the battle, we can see the movement of the Holy Spirit take over as the Lord works out the situation. This is also when you can talk over the situation with your parent or the adult in charge if you are not at home. When we talk things over, we again give the Holy Spirit an opportunity to speak through that person to give you some good advice on how to handle the situation.

Little lamb: I like talking things over with you. I am so ready for Jesus to come.

Adult sheep: While we wait, we learn that God's timing is so much better than our timing. God may not come when we want, but He is always on time. Our ancestors waited for over 2,000 years for Jesus to come, and when He came unto His own people, they did not receive Him but rejected him. They were not ready. Jesus is giving us every opportunity to be ready when He comes again. He will come when the time is right. (Add your comments or testimony.)

Let us pray together: Lord Jesus we know that your timing is always "on time." Holy Spirit help us to be patient as we wait for Jesus and help us to make wise decisions. Help us to know when to speak and when to be silent. (Add your Prayers and conclude with the closing prayer song.)

Closing prayer song:

COME, LORD JESUS. COME, LORD JESUS. COME, LORD JESUS. COME AND BE BORN IN OUR HEARTS.

DAY 13

Preparation: Read Proverbs chapter 13 and prepare the memory verse Proverbs chapter 13: verse 3.

Opening prayer song:

COME, HOLY SPIRIT. COME, HOLY SPIRIT. COME, HOLY SPIRIT. COME AND BE BORN IN OUR HEARTS.

Read the memory verse from your family Bible, Proverbs chapter 13: verse 3. Use the procedure for memorization highlighted in green in the introduction to help to memorize the scripture.

Adult sheep: As we wait for the coming of Jesus thinking before we speak and guarding the words that come out of our mouths is very important. Hurting words do their damage, and even when we try, we cannot take them back. We are to put a guard on our lips and ask God to let the words of our mouths and the meditations of our hearts be acceptable to him. Talk too much and you may get yourself into trouble and this may be your downfall. Be like the wise old owl and listen more and you will be better informed when you do speak.

Little lamb: I am waiting patiently and listening a lot. When is Jesus coming?

Adult sheep: You have been very patient and I am so proud of you. Jesus has left us many signs of His coming. Jesus says, "See that no one deceives you. Many will come in my name, saying I am he, and they will deceive many. When you hear of wars and rumors of wars and reports of wars, do not be alarmed; such things will happen, but it will not be the end. Nations will rise against nation and kingdom against kingdom. There will be earthquakes from place to place and there will be famines. These are the beginning of the labor pains." Doesn't this sound like things that are happening today? Jesus could come at any moment. We are preparing for His coming so that when He does come, we will be among those who are ready. (Add your comments or testimony.)

Adult sheep: You are really growing in wisdom. Let us pray together and ask the Holy Spirit to help us to be prepared when Jesus comes to us. Thank you Lord for the wisdom we are learning as we wait for Jesus to come. Thank you for helping us control the words that come out of our mouths. Thank you for helping us to listen more and speak words that are acceptable to God. Help us to truly be prepared when Jesus comes, today, tomorrow or at the end of time. (Add your prayers.)

Closing prayer song:

COME, LORD JESUS. COME, LORD JESUS. COME, LORD JESUS. COME AND BE BORN IN OUR HEARTS.

DAY 14

Preparation: Read Proverbs chapter 14 and prepare the memory verse, Proverbs chapter 14: verse 26.

Begin with the opening prayer song:

COME, HOLY SPIRIT. COME, HOLY SPIRIT. COME, HOLY SPIRIT. COME AND LEAD US TODAY.

Read Proverbs chapter 14: verse 26 from your family Bible. Use the procedure for memorization that is highlighted in green in the introduction to memorize the scripture verse for today.

Adult sheep: As we wait for the coming of Jesus, we are reminded about the importance of parents who respect and honor God. The word of God says, "If you respect the Lord, you and your children will have a strong fortress and a life-giving foundation that keeps you safe from deadly traps". We must strive to respect the Lord and do what is right and just. As we follow the ways of the Lord, we will be a good example to our children and it will help them to be strong and not easily fooled by the ways of the world. Those who follow the ways of the Lord will flourish and bloom where they are planted. They will do those things that leads to new life, not death.

Little lamb: I want to follow the ways of the Lord and I am so happy to have parents around me to help show me the way.

Adult sheep: Yes, we are all examples for someone to follow, and you never know when someone is looking at you as a role model. That is why preparing for the coming of Jesus is so very important. We can be a sign and witness for Jesus without even knowing it. That is why God gives us the Holy Spirit to live in us to help us along the way. (Add your comments or testimony.)

Let us pray together and ask the Holy Spirit to help us. Holy Spirit within us, lead us and guide us to make good decisions. Help us to be good examples and role models to others. As we wait for Jesus to come help us to grow, flourish and receive new life. (Add your prayers and then conclude with the closing prayer song.)

COME, LORD JESUS. COME, LORD JESUS. COME, LORD JESUS. COME AND BE BORN IN OUR HEARTS.

DAY 15

Preparation: Read Proverbs chapter 15 and prepare the memory verse and be ready to use the procedure highlighted in green in the introduction to memorize it. The memory verse for today is Proverbs chapter 15: verse 3.

Begin with the opening prayer song:

COME, HOLY SPIRIT. COME, HOLY SPIRIT. COME, HOLY SPIRIT. COME AND LEAD US TODAY.

Remember to always read the memory verse from your family Bible first Proverbs: chapter 15: verse 3. Then use the procedure highlighted in green in the introduction to assist in memorizing the memory verse.

Adult sheep: The Lord sees everything we do whether good or bad. He keeps watch over us all. He is our loving Father and He protects us also.

Little lamb: I don't know if I want God to see all that I do.

Adult sheep: Don't you want to be loved, protected, and cared for all of the time?

Little lamb: But what if I am caught doing wrong?

Adult sheep: If you are caught doing wrong and you are corrected, be smart and accept the correction. Children with a knowledge of God's presence and love make their parents happy and everyone with wisdom follows the straight path. It is also helpful to pray and ask for wisdom to make the right decisions. The Lord is disgusted with those who do wrong, but He loves everyone who does right. If you turn from the right way, you will be punished, and he who hates correction will die. (Add your comments and/or testimony.)

Let us pray together and ask the Holy Spirit to help us make good decisions. Thank you, God for being always with us. Holy Spirit help us to make good decisions and to the right things, so that we will not feel like we have to hide from God. We are aware of God's love for us shown through Jesus Christ, Your Son. As we wait for His coming help us to look at correction as a good thing, that will lead us to new life.

(Add your prayers and the close with the closing prayer song.)

COME, LORD JESUS. COME, LORD JESUS. COME, LORD JESUS. COME AND BE BORN IN OUR HEARTS.

DAY 16

Preparation: Read Proverbs Chapter 16 and make the memory verse strips, index cards, or poster. The memory verse for today is Proverbs chapter 16: verse 7.

Begin the day with the opening prayer song:

COME, HOLY SPIRIT. COME, HOLY SPIRIT. COME, HOLY SPIRIT. COME AND LEAD US TODAY.

Read Proverbs chapter 16: verse 7 from your family Bible. Complete the memory verse activity.

Adult sheep: As we wait for the coming of Jesus let us think about some of the benefits we receive when we strive to do things God's way. When the Lord is pleased with our ways, He makes even our enemies be at peace with us.

Little lamb: You mean even if someone is bullying me, God can make them be at peace with me and stop the bullying?

Adult sheep: Yes, all things are possible with God. But if someone is bullying you, you should tell the adult in charge about it and tell your parents. They will be helpful in bringing about peace and putting a stop to the bullying. God uses people to help us with our problems and you should not hesitate to ask for help.

Little lamb: I will ask for help when it is needed.

Adult sheep: Jesus came as a little baby dependent on Mary and Joseph to take care of him. One of the greatest gifts that God gives us is also parents who love and take care of us. We know that we are loved by God and God made everything for His own end. When we entrust our works to the Lord, our plans will succeed. We make our plans but the Lord decides where we will go. If we acknowledge God in all our ways, He will direct our steps. As always, we pray and ask for the help of the Holy Spirit to make the right choices. (Add your comments or testimony.)

Adult sheep: Let us pray together. Holy Spirit come with your wisdom and help us make the right choices in life. We want the Lord to be pleased with our ways. Lead us to ask for help when needed and to always know that our parents and God loves us very much. (Add your prayers and then conclude with the closing prayer song.)

COME, LORD JESUS. COME, LORD JESUS. COME, LORD JESUS. COME AND BE BORN INOUR HEARTS.

DAY 17

Preparation: Read Proverbs chapter 17, then make the memory strips, index cards, or poster with the memory verse, Proverbs 17: verse 13.

Begin with the opening prayer song:

COME, HOLY SPIRIT. COME, HOLY SPIRIT. COME, HOLY SPIRIT. COME AND LEAD US TO DAY.

Read Proverbs chapter 17: verse 13 from your family Bible. Use the procedure for memorization of scripture highlighted in green in the introduction.

Adult sheep: We remember as we wait for Jesus that we are not to be mean and do evil things to others.

Little lamb: We have talked a lot about overcoming evil with good but suppose someone continue to be mean to me?

Adult sheep: That's a good question! It says in our Bible verse we are not to return evil for good and if a person returns evil for good from his house evil will not depart. So, when one does evil things then evil will stay with them attracting more evil. In the same way if one does good it attracts more good and will overcome the evil. If you are doing the right things and someone continues to treat you badly, you should tell your parents or the person in charge but continue to not be resentful and evil to them. As we wait for Jesus we are to be forgiving and pray for those who despitefully use us. Bless those who curse you, call you names and do not be mean to them. You will keep your friends if you forgive them, but you will lose your friends if you keep talking about what they did wrong. (Add your comments or testimony.)

Adult sheep: Let us pray together and ask the Holy Spirit to help us. Holy Spirit help us to be forgiving and be able to overcome evil with good. We pray for those who have been hurtful to us and we ask the Lord to bless them and help them to change and become better people. (Add your own prayers.)

Closing prayer song:

COME, LORD JESUS. COME, LORD JESUS. COME, LORD JESUS. COME AND BE BORN IN OUR HEARTS.

DAY 18

Preparation: Read Proverbs chapter 18 and prepare the memory verse, Proverbs 18: 13.

Begin with the opening prayer song:

COME, HOLY SPIRIT. COME, HOLY SPIRIT. COME, HOLY SPIRIT. COME AND LEAD US TODAY.

Read the memory verse, Proverbs chapter 18: verse 13 from your family Bible. Using the procedure for memorization of scripture highlighted in green in the introduction go over the memory verse then the conversation begins.

Adult sheep: As we wait for the coming of Jesus be should be listening and watching for His coming.

Little lamb: I remember we talked about the wise old owl and how he was able to hear more because he wasn't talking all the time.

Adult sheep: Yes, some people talk all the time and are always so busy God cannot get their attention. Not only do they not listen but they hurry and make decisions without thinking things through. This can cause one to make bad decisions and can lead to many misunderstandings.

Little lamb: I feel really bad when I make wrong decisions.

Adult sheep: God does not want us to feel bad, and He is always available to help us. Therefore, we should take a minute to think before we speak and make our decisions. It can lead to shame and it can be embarrassing to give an answer before you listen. You are to make your words good and you will be glad that you did. Talk too much and you may have to eat the words that you say or they may get you into trouble. God loves us and is always there to help us if will be just take the time to stop and listen. Jesus is coming and we await His coming let us read the scriptures, pray, listen and watch for signs of His coming. (Add your comments or testimony.)

Let us pray together: Help us o Lord to take the time to listen for your voice. Help us be still and know that you will direct us, as we wait patiently with an open heart and mind. (Add your prayers.)

Sing the closing prayer song:

COME, LORD JESUS. COME, LORD JESUS. COME, LORD JESUS. COME AD BE BORN IN OUR HEARTS.

DAY 19

Preparation: Read Proverbs chapter 19 and prepare the memory verse. The memory verse is Proverbs chapter 19: verse 26.

Begin with the opening prayer song:

COME, HOLY SPIRIT. COME, HOLY SPIRIT. COME, HOLY SPIRIT. COME AND LEAD US TODAY.

Read the memory verse, Proverbs chapter 19: verse 26 from your family Bible. Use the procedure for memorization of scripture highlighted in green in the introduction to memorize the memory verse.

Adult sheep: Children who do not obey their parents shames them and violates God's Commands. We see that it is very important to control our temper as we wait for Jesus to come. When we are angry, we must stop, think and re-spond with love. Sometimes it is better not to respond at all. For if we want a more peaceful world, we must be kind and just to all people. We are more alive when we practice being loving and kind to others. We benefit ourselves because we are more peaceful and happy.

Little lamb: I want to be happy and I will respect my par-ents and be kind, but I also want Jesus to hurry and come!

Adult sheep: We are all wanting Jesus to come and He will come in due time. While we wait, we open up our hearts and minds to God and ask the Holy Spirit to grant us the gift of patience. To be patient is to endure discomfort without complaining or getting angry. It involves self-control, humil-ity, and generosity, all of which are virtues. So, you see that is why we pray and ask for the help of the Holy Spirit. We listen to counsel and receive instruction so that we can make good decisions and wait patiently for Jesus to come. (Add your comments or testimony.)

Let us pray together: Come, Holy Spirit and fill our hearts and help us to be respect our parents, be slow to anger and practice patience without complaining. Help us to have self-control, humility and generosity. (Add your prayers.)

Let us sing our closing prayer song:

COME, LORD JESUS. COME, LORD JESUS. COME, LORD JESUS. COME AND BE BORN IN OUR HEARTS.

DAY 20

Preparation: Read Proverbs chapter 20 and prepare the memory verse paper strips, index cards, or poster. The memory verse is Proverbs chapter 20: verse 11. On this day we will begin preparation for the Birthday Party for Jesus that will be held on the 25th day. It does not matter which month or day of the year this is, the party will be on the 25th day of your journey of waiting for Jesus. At the end of this day please talk about the birthday party, who to invite, send out invitations or save the date with the date, time and place for the party. On the 25th day the plan for the party is outlined, with room for your own touch to be given to the party. The plans will be simple and each day from now on there will be reminders about the birthday party until the 25th day.

Begin with the opening prayer song:

COME, HOLY SPIRIT. COME, HOLY SPIRIT. COME, HOLY SPIRIT. COME AND BE BORN IN OUR HEARTS.

Read the memory verse Proverbs chapter 20: verse 11 from your family Bible. Use the paper strips, index cards, or poster that you have prepared to teach the memory verse. The procedure is highlighted in green in the introduction. When you have completed this activity, the conversation begins.

Adult sheep: You can see that being good and having good manners is another way we can wait for Jesus and prepare the way for His coming. What you do early in life affects your moral character. Even children are known by their doings. You should want your work to be pure and right as we wait for Jesus to come.

Little lamb: Yes, but when is Jesus coming?

Adult sheep: No one knows the day or hour that Jesus will come. We celebrate His first coming on Christmas. In our country we celebrate the birth of Jesus on December 25. On our 25th day we are going to celebrate the birth of Jesus also. It may come on any month or day depending on the time when we started reading this book. On the 25th day we will have a Birthday Party for Jesus and be reminded about how Jesus came into the world.

As we wait for His coming, we are reminded today that the good or bad that children do, shows what they are like. If you want to be perceived as a good child you should do good things. To say please and thank you and have good manners will help others to see that your conduct is innocent and right. Whenever you receive a gift, do not forget to say thank you. Even if you do not particularly like the gift, be thankful that the person thought enough of you to give you a gift.

If you accidentally step on a person's toe or bump into them, you should say, "excuse me" or "I am sorry." This will let the person know that you didn't mean to hurt them. Even if they do not understand and are rude, you did what was right. We are not to let other peoples' reaction determine what we do. Practice good manners any way. (Add your comments or personal testimony.)

Adult sheep: We need the help of God and so now we pray together: Holy Spirit, God our Father, help us to make good decisions and practice good manners. We know that Jesus is coming and we want to be ready and prepared for His coming. (Add your prayers and then sing the closing prayer song.)

Closing prayer song:

COME, LORD JESUS. COME, LORD JESUS. COME, LORD JESUS. COME AND BE BORN INOUR HEARTS.

DAY 21

Preparation: Read Proverbs chapter 21 and prepare the memory verse. The memory verse is Proverbs chapter 21: verse 5. Remember we are also preparing for the Birthday Party for Jesus on the 25th day. At the end of today sit together and continue to make plans. Ask such questions as, "Have we send out or verbally invited people to come? Have we decided on a menu for the party?"

Begin with the opening prayer song:

COME, HOLY SPIRIT. COME, HOLY SPIRIT. COME, HOLY SPIRIT. COME AND BE BORN IN OUR HEARTS.

Read the memory verse Proverbs chapter 21: verse 5 from your family Bible. Use the procedure for memorization of scripture highlighted in green in the introduction to help our little lamb remember the memory verse.

Adult sheep: Planning and working hard is helpful to being a success in every area of our lives. We are preparing for the coming of Jesus, and as we wait, we are doing those things that will help us to be ready when He comes. We also, know not to hurry but to wait on the guidance of the Holy Spirit. Haste makes waste and may cause you to make mistakes. The Lord knows our hearts and doing what is right pleases the Lord more than making offerings to him.

Little lamb: I just want Jesus to come and I do want to do the right things.

Adult sheep: One thing we can do to stay on the right track, making the correct decisions is to ask, "What would Jesus do?" Jesus was quiet and He did not argue when someone came and tried to get Him upset. One time He wrote in the sand before answering and gave the people time to think before they acted. We are to do the same, let go and give God time to take over. The other thing we can always do is to pray. (Add your comments or testimony.)

Let us pray together: Holy Spirit, when we are tempted to hastily react to a situation, help us to remember what Jesus would do and act accordingly. Help us plan and work hard when we are trying to accomplish something. Help us to not be in a hurry but to take our time and do the job or activity in the right way. (Add your prayers.)

Then conclude with the closing prayer song:

COME, LORD JESUS. COME, LORD
JESUS. COME, LORD JESUS. COME
AND BE BORN IN OUR HEARTS.

DAY 22

Preparation: Read Proverbs chapter 22 and prepare the memory on paper strips, index cards, or on a poster. The memory verse for today is Proverbs chapter 22: verse 6. In preparation for the Birthday Party for Jesus be sure you have all the supplies needed and decide on what kind of cake you all want for the party. You may bake the cake or order one just be sure to have "Happy Birthday to Jesus" on the cake.

Begin with the opening prayer song:

COME, HOLY SPIRIT. COME, HOLY SPIRIT. COME, HOLY SPIRIT. COME AND LEAD US TODAY.

Read the memory verse Proverbs chapter 22: verse 6 from your family Bible. Use the procedure for memorization of scripture, highlighted in green in the introduction to help your little lamb remember the memory verse for today.

Adult sheep: It is the responsibility of your parents to train you in the way you should go. Children cannot raise themselves they need training from parents who are godly and are also waiting for the coming of Jesus. Loving parents can help children become loving adults. When you honor and obey your parents, you are promised a long happier life by God.

Little lamb: I am happy to obey my parents!

Adult sheep: I am happy that you are an obedient child and listen to your parents. We must also learn to listen to those in authority over us. Authority figures like teachers, preachers, and policemen should be respected and listened to. When you feel that something was done wrong to you, remember to go to your parents right away and let them know what happened. They will be able to handle the situation without you becoming disrespectful or receiving improper actions. We need the help from the Holy Spirit to make good choices as we journey through life. That is why we are to pray without ceasing. Prayer is our weapon and prayer changes things and work them out for our good. (Add your comments or testimony.)

Let us pray together: Come, Holy Spirit and help us to honor and obey our parents and those in authority. Help us to practice self-control and strive to be good. Help us to be peaceful and to think before we act and to let our parents know when we need help. (Add your prayers, then end with the closing prayer song.)

COME, LORD JESUS. COME, LORD JESUS. COME, LORD JESUS. COME AND BE BORN IN OUR HEARTS.

DAY 23

Preparation: Read Proverbs chapter 23 and make the paper strips, index cards, or poster with the memory verse. The memory verses for today are Proverbs chapter 23: verse 24.

In preparation for the birthday party for Jesus, make sure you have all the supplies that you need, paper plates, forks, etc. If you are going to give any little gifts to the children, such as candy, fruits, etc. check to see if you have enough for all the children invited with a few extras.

Begin with the opening prayer song:

COME, HOLY SPIRIT. COME, HOLY SPIRIT. COME, HOLY SPIRIT. COME AND LEAD US TODAY.

Read the memory verse for today, Proverbs, chapter 23: verse 24 from your family Bible. Use the procedure for memorization of scripture highlighted in green in the introduction to help your little lamb remember the memory verse for today.

Adult sheep: We are so happy when you make the right choices and decisions. God gave you to us as gift and we treasure you and want only the best for you. I know that when you follow God's way, you will have a happier and more peaceful life. You are blessed as you walk not in the counsel of the ungodly or in the way of sinners. It is also good to read and ponder the word of God to receive instruction. This will help you make wise decisions and your Father will greatly rejoice.

Little lamb: I want to make my parents happy and now I am eager for Jesus to come!

Adult sheep: Yes, we are eagerly waiting for Jesus to come. We are preparing the way for the Lord Jesus to come and find us ready for His coming. When He does come, we will be like a tree planted by a river, strong with deep roots, having wisdom, knowledge and understanding. We will be like a bride ready for her wedding prepared for the groom and celebration to come. I want you to always remember that God loves you and has given you the greatest gift of all, Jesus Christ our Lord. If we believe in him, we will not perish, but will have eternal life. (Add your comments or testimony.)

Adult sheep: We are to pray always and ask for the help of the Holy Spirit to have an open mind and spirit. Let us pray together: Holy Spirit lead us to a closer walk with Jesus. Help us to ponder on the word and let Jesus the Word come into our lives and save us. Thank you, Jesus for helping us make the right decisions. (Add your prayers and then conclude with the closing prayer song.)

COME, LORD JESUS. COME, LORD JESUS. COME, LORD JESUS. COME AND BE BORN IN OUR HEARTS.

DAY 24

Preparation: Read Proverbs chapter 24 and prepare the memory verse. The memory verse for today is Proverbs chapter 24: verse 16. Tomorrow is the Birthday Party for Jesus. Make sure you have everything that you need for the party. On tomorrow you and your little lamb will have your time together as usual before the party. You may look ahead to the outline for the party so that you both will be prepared when your guests arrive.

Opening prayer song:

COME, HOLY SPIRIT. COME, HOLY SPIRIT. COME, HOLY SPIRIT. COME AND LEAD US TODAY.

Read the memory verse Proverbs chapter 24: verse 16 from your family Bible. Use the procedure for memorization to help you both remember the scripture verse for today.

Adult sheep: Even good people striving to live God's way may stumble and fall, but they can get back up. But when trouble strikes the wicked, they will fall into mischief. When we fall down, we get back up, with the help of the Lord.

Little lamb: What happens if I make bad choices?

Adult sheep: You are a precious child of God. Made in His image and likeness, plus you are waiting, preparing for the coming of Jesus. When you stumble and fall, call on the Lord to help you get back up. He will never let you down. Jesus gave us a good example of this on His way to the cross. He fell three times, but He got back up to complete God's plan for His life. He had a purpose to fulfill and He kept going until He reached His destiny. He shed His blood for you, for me and for the whole world, so that we could be saved.

Little lamb: What if I do something really, really bad?

Adult sheep: All sin is bad and can lead one to destruction. We must believe in God's love and plan for us. Remember Jesus did not come into the world to condemn the world but so that we are saved through our faith in him. When we fall, do bad things, or when we sin, we are to get up and run to Jesus and ask for forgiveness. Don't ever feel that you have done something so wrong that He won't forgive you. So, continue to get back up and ask Jesus to forgive you and believe that it is done. He will never leave us or forsake us. (Add your comments or testimony.)

Let us pray together: Come, Holy Spirit and lead us to believe in God's unconditional love for us and that nothing can separate us from His love. When we fall, help us to get back up and ask for forgiveness and continue on our journey. (Add your prayers and conclude with the closing prayer song.)

COME, LORD JESUS. COME, LORD JESUS. COME, LORD JESUS. COME AND BE BORN INOUR HEARTS.

DAY 25

Preparation: This is the day of the "Birthday Party for Jesus. You will read Proverbs chapter 25 and prepare the memory verse. The memory verse for today is Proverbs chapter 25: verse 25. You will complete the session for today with your little lamb before the party. Later in the day the party will begin with the invited guest. At the end of this session is the outline for the birthday party. You may have cake and punch or add pizza or any refreshments that you can afford. At the end of the party you may give out a treat or memory card to the children. This is your party and your opportunity to tell the story of the birth of Jesus. Keep things simple and only do what you can afford.

Begin with the opening prayer song:

COME, HOLY SPIRIT. COME, HOLY SPIRIT. COME, HOLY SPIRIT. COME AND LEAD US TODAY.

Read the memory verse Proverbs chapter 25: verse 25 from your family Bible. Use the procedure for memorization of scripture to help remember the memory verse for today. Then the conversation begins:

Adult sheep: In our memory verse we learned that good news from far away refreshes like cold water when you are thirsty. If you have been out in the heat and come inside and someone gives you a glass of cold water you know how refreshing it is. Well we have been waiting for Jesus to come and today we receive the "Good News" about the birth of Jesus, His first coming. His coming is so refreshing to us that we want to share this news with others. That is why we are having the Birthday Party for Jesus. We will share the story of the birth of Jesus and talk about the reading. We will let our invited guests ask questions, or if they are quiet, we can ask questions to help them remember the birth of Jesus. We will pray a prayer to ask Jesus who brings us good news about God's love for us to come and give us a refreshing drink of His living water. Then we will sing happy birthday to Jesus and cut the birthday cake. (Add your comments.)

Little lamb: May I cut the birthday cake?

Adult sheep: Yes, you may cut the cake and help with the games and singing. We want everyone to feel welcomed and have a great time.

Let us pray together: Thank you Lord for today and for all of your blessings. Help us to have a wonderful Birthday

Party for Jesus. Help us to see His comings as truly refreshing life giving "good news." (Add your personal prayers.)

Closing prayer song:

COME, LORD JESUS. COME, LORD JESUS. COME, LORD JESUS. COME AND BE BORN IN OUR HEARTS.

Outline for the
Birthday Party for Jesus

Welcome everyone and help them feel comfortable.

After everyone has arrived have everyone introduce themselves and tell something about themselves; maybe their favorite color.

Tell them this is a birthday party for Jesus and we want everyone to celebrate with us.

Pray a prayer to welcome the Holy Spirit or you can sing the Come, Holy Spirit song.

Tell everyone we have some refreshing "Good News" to tell them.

Read Luke chapter 2: verses 1-7 from your family Bible.

(After the reading)

Adult sheep: This good news is refreshing to everyone, especially to those who have been waiting for Jesus to come.

The good news about the birth of Jesus tells us this happened in a faraway country. Have you ever been thirsty and someone gives you a cool drink of water? How refreshing that was and it made you feel good inside. We have feelings like that on today as we celebrate the birth of Jesus. Mary and Joseph had to travel to be enrolled, counted in their own hometown. So they traveled from Galilee, from the town of Nazareth to Judea, to the city of David, that is called Bethlehem. Mary and Joseph would have been happy to receive a cool drink of water but there no room for them at the inn and no one gave them a drink. Jesus was born in a stable, a place where animals are kept. Mary wrapped Him in swaddling clothes and laid Him in a manger. Jesus was not born in a palace but in a stable. He became one with us and He can identify with the rich and the poor. The Bible tells us that God so loved the world that He gave His only begotten Son so that all who believed in Him could be saved through His shed blood on the cross. He died so that we may live. That is why His birth is such refreshing, "Good news." (Add your comments or testimony.)

Does anyone have any questions? If no one has questions, you may ask some, such as:

1. Where was Jesus born?
2. What is His mother's name?
3. Why did Jesus come into the world?

We have been preparing for the coming of Jesus by singing, praying and reading scripture. Before we sing Happy Birthday and cut the cake and have refreshments let us pray a prayer and ask Jesus to come and refresh us and help us to grow in our love for him.

Let us pray together: Come, Lord Jesus and be our Savior, save us from all sin and refresh us, help us to grow in our love for God and all others.

(Add your own prayers.)

Sing together: Joy to the World

(If you feel that they will not know the words, provide the words for them to sing from.)

After the song, cut the cake and sing Happy Birthday to Jesus. You may play any games that you feel are appropriate at this time. As the children leave give them something to help them remember this day. (Maybe a copy of the memory verse or John 3:16.

DAY 26

Preparation: Read Proverbs chapter 26. Prepare the memory verse on paper strips, index cards, or poster. Proverbs chapter 26: verse 14.

Opening prayer song:

COME, HOLY SPIRIT. COME, HOLY SPIRIT. COME, HOLY SPIRIT. COME AND LEAD US TODAY.

Read the memory verse Proverbs chapter 26: verse 14 from your family Bible. Use the procedure for memorization to help you little lamb remember the memory verse. Then the conversation begins.

Adult sheep: The slothful, lazy person will stay in bed and turn over. The wise person will be about doing God's will for their lives. Yesterday we had our birthday party for Jesus and today be should still be excited about the birth of Jesus that we want to continue to tell others about His coming. The angels came with a message that sank into the hearts of the shepherds. "Do not be afraid. I bring you good news of great joy that will be for all people." Jesus wants to take away our fears. When things are strange and out of the ordinary, we are to trust God and do not fear. The angels continued, for today in the city of David, a Savior has been born unto you, who is Messiah and Lord. We must not forget that Jesus is our Savior and Lord and put Him first in our lives. The angels began to praise and give glory to God as they said, "Glory to God in the highest and on earth peace to those on whom His favor rests. We should give glory and praise to God for His favor rests upon us. When hearing and accepting the good news about the birth of Jesus, we, too, must not be lazy and roll over in bed we are to get up and praise God for the greatest gift on earth. Like the angels going to the shepherds we are to tell others about the love of God shown to us through Jesus Christ and His lowly birth.

Little lamb: I heard the "Good News" about the birth of Jesus and I enjoyed the birthday party for Jesus. Now like the angels, I give praise and glory to God. The angels went to the shepherds with this good news and I must go to tell others about Jesus.

Adult sheep: Yes, we believe and have received Jesus into our lives and hearts, we too sing glory to God in the highest as we continue to celebrate the coming of Jesus Christ. We continue to tell others about Jesus and why He came into the world. We will not be lazy and think only of ourselves, but we will go tell it on the mountains, that Jesus Christ is born.

Let us pray together: Thank you Lord Jesus for coming into the world and into our lives. Help us to give you glory and praise as we strive to grow in our love for God and all others. Give us the grace and courage to tell others about Jesus. (Add your prayers.)

Closing prayer song:

COME, LORD JESUS. COME, LORD JESUS. COME, LORD JESUS. COME AND BE BORN INOUR HEARTS.

DAY 27

Preparation: Read Proverbs chapter 27. Prepare the memory verse Proverbs chapter 27: verse 2 on paper strips, index cards, or poster.

Opening prayer song:

COME, HOLY SPIRIT. COME, HOLY SPIRIT. COME, HOLY SPIRIT. COME AND LEAD US TODAY.

Read the memory verse Proverbs chapter 27: verse 2 from your family Bible. Use the procedure for memorization to help your child or children remember the verse for today.

Adult sheep: In our memory verse we talked about not praising yourself but let others praise you. The angels went to the shepherds and gave glory and praise to God for the coming of Jesus. The shepherds went in haste to see what the Lord had made known to them. They found everything just like the angels told them. They returned to their sheep praising God and saying wonderful things about God. Those who heard the shepherds wondered about what the shepherd told them. The shepherds praised and gave glory to God not themselves. They made known abroad the sayings which were told them concerning this child. We are to share what we know about Jesus to others also.

Little lamb: Wasn't the shepherds considered to be poor people at that time?

Adult sheep: They were chosen to show that Jesus came for all people, even those who are considered poor or lower class. We are all receivers of God's mercy and love. All we have to do is receive what God has already given and to give the praise and glory to God, not to ourselves or anyone else. We are saved by grace so that no one can boast. If you are doing good even strangers will see and praise you. Jesus has come into the world set us free from sin and destruction. Glory and praise to God for giving us His Son, Jesus Christ our Lord.

Let us pray together: Lord Jesus, thank you for coming into the world to be our Savior. Help us to open our hearts and our lives to you. Holy Spirit come and teach us to love and praise God above all else. (Add your own prayers.)

Closing prayer song:

COME, LORD JESUS. COME, LORD
JESUS. COME, LORD JESUS. COME
AND BE BORN IN OUR HEARTS.

DAY 28

Preparation: Read Proverbs chapter 28 and prepare the memory verse Proverbs chapter 28: verse 6 on paper strips, index cards, or poster.

Opening prayer song:

COME, HOLY SPIRIT. COME, HOLY SPIRIT. COME, HOLY SPIRIT. COME AND LEAD US TODAY. ///

Read the memory verse Proverbs chapter 28: verse 6 from your family Bible. Use the procedure for memorization of scripture that is highlighted in green in the introduction to help your little lamb remember the memory verse for today.

Adult sheep: We see that it is better to be poor and live right than to be rich and dishonest. The shepherds may have been poor but they were honest and willing to tell others about Jesus. Mary and Joseph were obedient to the law and took Jesus up to the temple to present Jesus to the Lord. He was circumcised and given the name Jesus.

Little lamb: Mary and Joseph named their baby Jesus why?

Adult sheep: The name of Jesus was given to Him by the angel Gabriel when he said to Mary, "Behold you shall conceive in your womb and bear a son, and you shall name Him Jesus." Jesus was consecrated to the Lord as the law required. Being obedient to God and His word is better than offering to the Lord a sacrifice. Jesus has come and we are so happy and like the shepherds and Mary and Joseph we are to obey the rules of God. This will help us to live a long happy life with the wisdom that comes from God.

Little lamb: I am so glad that we prepared for the coming of Jesus and now that we have celebrated His birth I want to go on living and learning how to continue to wait for Jesus.

Adult sheep: Yes, Jesus is coming again and we do not know the day or the hour so we continue to prepare for His coming. It could be any day, even today. We strive to walk in honesty and integrity always knowing that we have the Holy Spirit as our helper and guide. (Add your comments or testimony.)

Adult sheep: Let us pray together and ask for the help of the Holy Spirit. Holy Spirit come and help us to be obedient and live a life that will help us to be ready when Jesus comes again. (Add your Prayers.)

Closing prayer song:

COME, LORD JESUS. COME, LORD JESUS. COME, LORD JESUS. COME AND BE BORN IN OUR HEARTS.

DAY 29

Preparation: Read Proverbs chapter 29 and prepare the memory verse, Proverbs chapter 29: verse 18 on paper strips, index cards, or poster.

Begin with the opening prayer song:

COME, HOLY SPIRIT. COME, HOLY SPIRIT. COME, HOLY SPIRIT. COME AND LEAD US TODAY.

Read the memory verse, Proverbs chapter 29: verse 18 from your family Bible. Use the procedure for memorization of scripture to help your little lamb remember the scripture verse for today.

Adult sheep: In our memory verse we see how God blesses and makes happy those who obey the law and are guided by the Holy Spirit. Simeon was a just and devout man who believed in the coming of the Messiah and waited for Him to come; the Holy Spirit was upon him. Simeon had been waiting for a long time, he believed in the prophecy and God blessed him. He came into the temple guided by the Spirit, and when the parents of Jesus brought Him into the temple, Simeon was able to take Jesus into his arms and blessed God. We too, believe that Jesus Christ will come again and we await His coming. We will be guided by the Spirit and do what is right and will be blessed as we wait for His second coming.

Little lamb: I am so happy that Jesus came as a little baby like me and I am so glad that He is coming again.

Adult sheep: Yes, that is why we continue to prepare for His coming and strive to be ready when He comes. Let us pray together: Thank you Lord Jesus for coming as a little baby to be our Savior and Lord, help us to live for you and obey your commands. Help us to make the world a better place as we await your second coming. (Add your prayers.)

Sing the closing prayer song:

COME, LORD JESUS. COME, LORD JESUS. COME, LORD JESUS. COME AND BE BORN IN OUR HEARTS.

DAY 30

Preparation: Read Proverbs chapter 30 and prepare the memory verse paper strips, index cards, or poster. The memory verse is Proverbs chapter 30: verse 5.

Opening prayer song:

COME, HOLY SPIRIT. COME, HOLY SPIRIT. COME, HOLY SPIRIT. COME AND LEAD US TODAY.

Read the memory verse Proverbs chapter 30: verse 5 from your family Bible. Use the procedure for memorization of scripture highlighted in green in the introduction to help your little lamb remember the memory verse for today.

Adult sheep: We must remember that everything God said is true and we can always come to Him for safety. He is a shield to those who put their trust in him. Anna, a widow of great age never left the temple. She trusted God and was there to serve God with fastings and prayers night and day. She saw Mary and Joseph and the baby Jesus and gave thanks and praise to God and told others about the child Jesus. Mary and Joseph having fulfilled all the prescription of the law returned to Nazareth. The child grew in wisdom and the favor of God was upon him.

Little lamb: I want to be like Jesus and be wise and have God's favor!

Adult sheep: That is why we have been spending this time in preparation for the coming of Jesus. We too want to be wise and grow in God's favor. Anna and Simeon were in the temple and they were able to see Jesus. It is good to be in the house of the Lord. The word of God is pure and He is a shield to those who trust in him. We have also asked the Holy Spirt to be with us to lead us and guide us each day.

Let us pray together. Come, Holy Spirit and help us to grow in wisdom and in favor with God and man. Help us to be at the right place and time to see Jesus when He comes again. (Add your own prayers.)

Closing prayer song:

COME, LORD JESUS. COME, LORD JESUS. COME, LORD JESUS. COME AND BE BORN IN OUR HEARTS.

DAY 31

Preparation: Read Proverbs chapter 31 and prepare the memory verse on paper strips, index cards, or poster. The memory verse is Proverbs chapter 31: verse 31.

Opening prayer song:

COME, HOLY SPIRIT. COME, HOLY SPIRIT. COME, HOLY SPIRIT. COME AND LEAD US TODAY.

Read the memory verse, Proverbs chapter 31: verse 31 from your family Bible. Use the procedure for memorization of scripture, highlighted in green in the introduction to help your little lamb remember the memory verse for today.

Adult sheep: We see that beauty fades away and charm can be deceiving but the woman who fears and honors the Lord deserves to be praised. We talked early on about the beginning of wisdom is to fear and honor God. Remember the Bible story about Jesus staying behind in the temple and Mary and Joseph did not know this until they missed Him and went back looking for him. They found Him in the temple, sitting in the midst of the doctors, both listening to them and asking them questions. When they saw him, they were amazed and Mary said to him, "Son, why have you done this to us? Your father and I have been looking for you with great anxiety." And He said to them, "Why are you looking for me? Did you not know that I must be in my Father's house?" He went down with them and came to Nazareth and was obedient to them; and Mary kept all these things in her heart. Jesus grew in wisdom and age and in favor with God and man.

Little lamb: I want to be like Jesus and grow in wisdom and in favor with God and man!

Adult sheep: Yes, we both want to grow in wisdom, in age and in favor with God and man that is why we have spent this time to prepare for the coming of Jesus. We learned that being wise will help us to live a long happier life and make good decisions along the way. Jesus went back with His family and was obedient to them. We also learned that obedience is better than to make promises and sacrifices to the Lord. We end as we began, renewing our commitment to Jesus and asking Him to be our Lord and Savior. We ask God for the grace to stay awake, so that we can be ready whenever Jesus comes.

Let us pray together and ask the Holy Spirit to help us: Holy Spirit come and fill us each day. Please, open our hearts, minds and spirits to the grace of God freely given to us through Jesus Christ and His shed blood on the cross. Help us to be obedient to God and listen to His word. Help us to apply the word of God to our everyday lives. Help us to be ready when Jesus returns. It could be today. Come, Lord Jesus!

(Add your own prayers.)

Closing prayer song:

COME, LORD JESUS. COME, LORD JESUS. COME, LORD JESUS. COME AND BE BORN IN OUR HEARTS.

Conclusion

The purpose of this book is to get the adult reader into the book of Proverbs because Proverbs come from God and He can be trusted to help us become wise and learn how to actively wait for the coming of His Son, Jesus. One verse is chosen for the adult sheep and little lamb to memorize and have a conversation about the verse, especially how to put the ideas from the verse into action in their everyday lives. This will help them be prepared for Jesus whenever He comes.

We know that Jesus is coming and that we celebrate His coming on December 25th each year. That is why I have used the opportunity on the 25th day to have a birthday party for Jesus. Telling the story about Jesus coming as a baby is very important for children to know. They should know why He came and also know to look forward to His coming again.

I ask the adult to read the whole chapter each day before beginning the conversation to help them accomplish reading the whole book of Proverbs. They may have other insights or comments from the chapter that they feel are important to share with their little lamb. This will make the sharing of comments at the end of each conversation more meaningful to the little lamb, especially when there is a testimony. This gives the Holy Spirit the opportunity to speak through them to the children. Faith grows through hearing the word of God and applying the truths to our lives.

Our children live in a world where the spiritual warfare is going on fiercely and they need wisdom to make the right decisions and choices to live a happy and productive life. There is an opening and closing prayer song asking for the help of the Holy Spirit and for Jesus to come into our hearts. We need the word of God and prayer to help us put on the armor of God with the ability to wait in faith for Jesus to return.

I hope that the adults and children who pick up this book and become engaged in the scriptures, prayers, and conversations will grow in their wisdom, knowledge, and understanding of God's love for them. And that they will put into action the truths that they learn from the Proverbs.

My desire is that their faith will grow, that they will have a better attitude about life, and that they will be better prepared for the coming of Jesus. Stay awake! Be prepared! This may be the day! COME, LORD JESUS!

ABOUT THE AUTHOR

Beatrice (Bea) Cunningham has been able to follow her dream of being a teacher as she admired her third-grade teacher and wanted to be like her. She grew up in Beaumont, Texas, graduated from Charlton-Pollard High School. She received a Bachelor of Science Degree in Elementary Education from Prairie View University, Prairie View, Texas. Later she graduated from the University of St. Thomas, Houston, Texas with a Master's Degree in Religious Education. She has also completed the formation training for Spiritual Directors/Companions from the Cenacle Retreat House in Houston, Texas.

Her career as a teacher has been in schools in the Diocese of Galveston-Houston for sixteen years. She has served as an Associate Director in the Catechetical Office of the Archdiocese of Galveston-Houston for another sixteen years, before retiring or redirecting her energy. In this capacity she has written articles and conducted workshops and seminars.

She is now residing at a Senior Care Community in Houston where she went with her husband who was ill and he died immediately after they arrived. She decided to stay because of the peaceful environment and Warren Chapel where she was when she received the inspiration for this book.

She is the mother of three children—one son who is deceased and two adult daughters. She has five grandchildren and six great-grandchildren and the count keeps on growing. She loves reading, singing, and praying for her family and others and considers herself a prayer warrior.